Handwriting With
Sight Words

Grade 2

by Lori Taylor

Published by
Frank Schaffer Publications®

Author: Lori Taylor

Editor: Linda Triemstra

Frank Schaffer Publications®

Send all inquiries to:
Frank Schaffer Publications
3195 Wilson Drive NW
Grand Rapids, Michigan 49534

Handwriting With Sight Words—grade 2

ISBN 0-7682-3442-5

1 2 3 4 5 6 7 8 9 MAZ 10 09 08 07 06

Table of Contents

Introduction

Handwriting is an important skill for children to learn and practice on a daily basis. Learning the fundamentals of handwriting makes everyday writing and schoolwork easier for children. The purpose of this book is to teach children the basic skills of handwriting using common sight words. The lessons are designed to be short and to teach the correct formation of letters. Make sure children work slowly to help develop their neatness, speed, and confidence as writers.

This book teaches capital letters, lowercase letters, some phonetic skills, and sight words. Some letters can be harder to learn than others. Harder ones typically seem to be those with diagonal lines, those that can be reversed, and those with letters that change directions when being practiced. Capital letters are usually easier for children since they are all the same height, start at the top line, and are usually easier to recognize. This book will start with capital letters first.

Model a few important habits for children to see before they begin practicing their letters. Have children check the height of the desk or table they are sitting at. It should be comfortable and steady for the child. Make sure children have both feet on the floor. Their heads should be relaxed and they should not be hunched over the page or leaning into the paper. Have children check the placement of their paper. It should be centered in front of the child and in a comfortable working position. The writing hand should rest below the printing area. The other hand might be "holding the paper" at the top or resting comfortably next to the paper. Right-handed students should place their hand at the top of the right corner, and left-handed students should place their hand at the top left corner.

It's also important for children to hold their pencil correctly. The pencil is like a tool. If children know how to hold it correctly, it works better. Almost all children will learn to hold the pencil correctly if they are shown the proper grip. The tip of the pencil should be held between the thumb and two fingers. The pencil can rest on the index finger or the ring finger, whichever feels most comfortable. Most people prefer the index finger. The eraser should be angled toward the child's shoulder. Encourage children to hold the pencil comfortably and not apply too much pressure. Some children use pencil grips to help with learning the proper grip. These can be found at most office supply stores and teacher stores.

Introduction

The pages in this book are designed for demonstration. Don't send children off to work on pages until you have demonstrated how to make the letters. Show children how to make each letter. Have children practice in the air or on their desk with a finger before practicing with paper and pencil. Many children need to "feel" the letter formation with their body before they are ready to actually write. Encourage children to take their time and really learn how to write the letters. Reward good letter formation and students who take their time.

Finally, have fun with handwriting! It's different from most subjects you teach. It's much like learning to ride a bike. Children keep practicing until they become naturals!

Shown below are letters with arrows indicating the direction of strokes used in forming each letter. You may follow this approach or use one of your own.

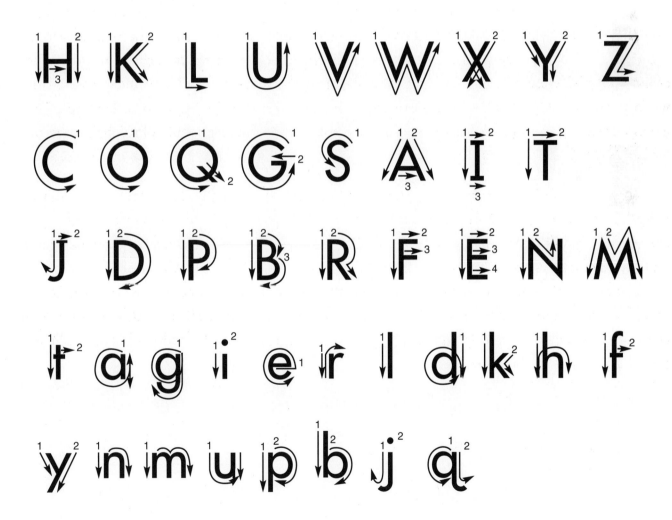

Capitals That Start in the Corner

Many capitals start in the upper left corner. This means that you will begin these letters with your pencil in the upper left corner. All of these letters are written below.

Let's practice making some of these together. We will start with *H*, *K*, and *L*.

Watch your teacher write each one. Then you try.

H

K

L

Corner Capitals

Let's try some more corner capitals. Watch your teacher write them first. Then you try.

U

V

W

X

Y

Z

Capitals That Start in the Center

Some capitals start in the center. Some are round like an apple. Let's try these ones first! Watch your teacher write a few. Then you try on your own.

The C starts at the top and curves to the left, but it doesn't close.

C

Now let's try the O. It starts like the C, but it goes all the way around.

O

The Q is an O with a tail.

Q

Let's try the G. It starts like the C, but then it ends with a center tail.

G

Center Capitals

There are five more center capitals: *S, A, I , T*, and J.

The *S* starts at the center and curves around, much like a snake.

S

The *A* starts at the center with two diagonal lines, and they are connected by a small horizontal line.

A

The I is a line written straight down and is given a short top and bottom.

I

The *T* is a line written straight down and is given a long top.

T

The J starts like a *T*, but then curves into a hook at the bottom and is given a long top.

J

More Capitals That Start in the Corner

Start these letters with your pencil in the upper left corner.

Let's start with the D. It starts at the top in the corner and goes down. Then you make a big bubble in front.

D _____

For P we start like D with a straight line, but then we add only half a bubble in front.

P _____

Start with a straight line for B, then add two half bubbles in front.

B _____

Start with the straight line for R, add a half bubble, and then add a short diagonal line.

R _____

More Corner Capitals

Place your pencil in the corner to start these letters.

An *F* starts with a straight line and has two lines branching off of it like a tree.

F _____

An *E* is just like an *F*, but with three branches coming off of it.

E _____

To make an *N*, start with a straight line, then make a diagonal line down to the right, and end with a line going straight up.

N _____

For *M*, start with a line that is slanted slightly to the left. Go back to the starting point and draw a line slanted slightly right, then draw a slanted line up from that point, then one more slanted line to the right to finish it.

M _____

Congratulations! You've learned all the capitals!

Name_____ Date _____

Review of Capitals

Let's review capital letters. Write each one three times.

H

K

L

U

V

W

X

Y

Z

C

O

Q

G

0-7682-3442-5 *Handwriting With Sight Words*

Review of Capitals

Write each capital letter three times.

S

A

I

T

J

D

P

R

F

E

N

M

Capital and Lowercase Letters That Are the Same

Many lowercase letters look the same as the matching capital letters.

The lowercase letters are just smaller and start at the middle line. Look at them below.

C O S V W X Z

Practice writing each letter below.

c _____

o _____

s _____

v

w _____

x _____

z _____

Identical Capital and Lowercase Letters

Below are the letters that have identical capital and lowercase letters. Practice writing each pair of letters.

C c _____

O o _____

S s _____

V v _____

Ww _____

X x _____

Z z _____

Name_____ Date _____

Lowercase t

Let's try the lowercase *t*. Start just above the middle line and go straight down. Then cross your lowercase *t* above the middle line.

t

to

it

two

too

cost

Published by Frank Schaffer Publications. Copyright protected.   0-7682-3442-5 *Handwriting With Sight Words*

Lowercase t

Look at the words in the *t* tree. Write the word that best fits into the blank for each sentence.

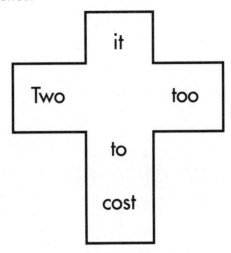

it

Two   too

to

cost

1. _____ girls went walking to the store.

2. The dog ran _____ catch the bone.

3. The little boy wanted to go to the store _____.

4. The sky was dark so they knew _____ would rain.

5. The candy _____ $1.00.

Hint: The word "too" means also.

Name_____ Date _____

Lowercase a

Let's try the lowercase a. The lowercase *a* starts like a *c* but goes up to the
middle line for a bump and then comes back down.

a

saw

as

at

cat

sat

was

Published by Frank Schaffer Publications. Copyright protected.   0-7682-3442-5 *Handwriting With Sight Words*

Lowercase a

Find the lowercase *a* words in the word search below. Use the words in the word bank.

was   cat

sat   at

saw   as

w	a	s	t	m	e	f	g	c
q	u	a	i	f	r	h	n	a
s	p	w	c	n	m	x	j	t
a	t	h	k	l	l	m	b	m
t	b	m	u	i	u	a	c	v
y	y	b	f	d	c	q	e	r
a	s	a	w	e	r	t	y	u

Name _____ Date _____

Lowercase g

Let's try the lowercase *g*. This letter is written just like the *a* except that it adds a tail at the bottom.

g

go

good

got

goat

wag

Lowercase g

Read the short story below. Underline all the words that have a lowercase *g*.

Lots of people have a dog for a pet. Dogs are very loyal friends. They love to learn tricks, play fetch, and give big, wet kisses. Dogs show they are happy by wagging their tails. Dogs can also help people. Some dogs can be trained to help people who are blind. Dogs are great pets!

Write a sentence using a word that has a lowercase *g* on the lines below.

_____

- -

_____

- -

_____

- -

_____

Name _____ Date _____

Lowercase i

Lowercase *i* is a straight line that starts on the middle line and ends on the bottom line. Then it is topped off with a dot above the middle line.

i

is

it

said

did

six

sit

Lowercase i

Look at the words on the inchworm. Write each word from the inchworm on the correct line below.

said   did   six

sit   is   It

1. "I want to go too," _____ Mary.

2. There are _____ people in my family.

3. The usher told us to _____ here for the play.

4. I _____ my homework yesterday.

5. She _____ in my second-grade class.

6. _____ is lunch time!

Lowercase e

Let's try lowercase e. It starts between the middle and bottom lines, then it bumps up to the middle line and curves around to the bottom line.

e

eat

get

we

see

give

Lowercase e

Write the words from the racetrack in ABC order on the lines below.

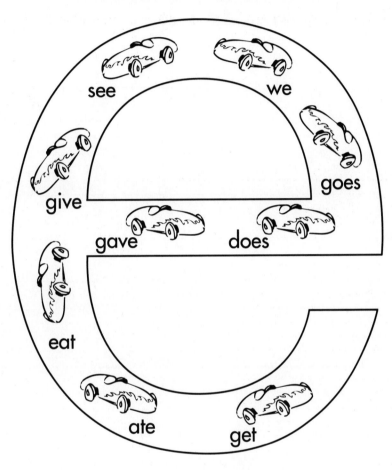

see   we   goes   give   gave   does   eat   ate   get

1. _____   6. _____

2. _____   7. _____

3. _____   8. _____

4. _____   9. _____

5. _____

Lowercase r

The lowercase *r* starts with a line straight down from the middle line. It comes back up and over to make a little hook.

r

ride

or

over

were

are

write

read

red

Lowercase r

Pick five words from page 26. Write a sentence for each word below.

1. _____

2. _____

3. _____

4. _____

5. _____

Draw a picture to go with one of your sentences.

Lowercase l

The lowercase *l* starts at the top line and goes straight down to end on the bottom line.

l

let

all

little

well

call

tell

Lowercase 1

Read the sentences below. Complete the puzzle using the words in the Word Bank.

Down

1. I am the opposite of big.

2. I am the opposite of young.

3. Everything or everyone.

4. The power to decide what to do and keep wanting to do it.

Across

1. To allow or permit.

4. A deep hole that is made to get water.

5. To say or put into words.

6. To ask or order to come.

Word Bank

will	all
old	call
tell	let
little	well

Lowercase d

Let's make the lowercase *d*. Lowercase *d* starts just like an *a*, but then it goes all the way up the top line and then comes back down.

d

do

dad

sad

was

as

dig

Lowercase d

Write each sentence below. Start each one with a capital letter and end each one with a period.

1. A goat ate green grass.

2. I saw two little cows.

3. Dad saw six cats.

4. Rags is a little dog.

5. Two dogs ate good treats.

Lowercase k

Making a lowercase *k* is like kicking. It starts like an *l*, then kicks up to the middle line and then kicks down to the bottom line.

k

kick

look

like

take

walk

skate

ask

work

Name_____ Date _____

Lowercase k

Use each word from the Word Bank in the sentences below.

Word Bank		
Look	like	walk
ask	kick	skate

I. _____ at all the beautiful flowers.

2. The boy can _____ the soccer ball.

3. We went for a _____ in the woods.

4. I _____ all kinds of fruit.

5. I will _____ my mom if I can go too.

6. My brother can _____ on the ice.

Lowercase h

An *h* starts like an *l*, but it comes back up to the middle line and then curves around and down to the bottom line.

h

how

her

he

what

with

white

his

the

had

which

those

where

Lowercase h

Look at the letter below. Notice that it starts with a greeting (Dear, Hello) and ends with a closing (Sincerely, Love, Your friend). Write the letter on the lines below.

Dear Ted,

We will see each other soon at school. I will have my

skates for recess. I love to skate. What do you think we will

read at school? Who is your teacher? See you soon.

Sincerely,

Rex

Lowercase f

The lowercase *f* is different from most letters. It starts at the top, but it curves to the left and then goes straight down. Then it is crossed like a *t*.

f

of

for

first

fast

after

Lowercase f

Look at the pairs of rhyming words.
Write the words on the lines below.

fish   dish

fold   cold

---

five   hive

fall   call

---

fast   past

fit   pit

---

fur   purr

fat   cat

Name_____ Date _____

Lowercase y

A lowercase y is like a monkey sitting in a tree with its tail hanging down. Start at the middle line and slant down to the bottom line. Then start at the middle line again and go down past the bottom line to make a tail.

y

you   very

away   yes

fly   say

they   yellow

0-7682-3442-5 *Handwriting With Sight Words*

Name_____ Date_____

Lowercase y

Help Joey the monkey put his bananas in ABC order.

very

always

funny

yes

try

carry

every

why

today

say

1. _____

2. _____

3. _____

4. _____

5. _____

6. _____

7. _____

8. _____

9. _____

10. _____

Lowercase n

Let's make a lowercase *n*. Lowercase *n* starts at the middle line with a straight line down, comes back up to make a hump, and then ends on the bottom line.

n

now   into

when   new

ten   not

open   seven

once   never

Name_____ Date _____

Lowercase n

Look at the birds flying around. Decide which short vowel sound each word
makes. Then write each word in the correct short vowel nest.

Published by Frank Schaffer Publications. Copyright protected.   0-7682-3442-5 *Handwriting With Sight Words*

Lowercase m

The lowercase *m* is written just like the *n*,
except it has another hump, like a camel.

m

small

myself

some

from

much

made

my

came

make

come

Lowercase m

Read the words with lowercase *m*. Decide if the vowel sound is long or short in each word. Write each word under the long or short side of the *m*.

Word Bank

make	made	small	my
	may	come	him
am	came	them	me

Long vowels

_____

_____

_____

_____

_____

_____

Short vowels

_____

_____

_____

_____

_____

_____

Lowercase u

Lowercase *u* is an upside-down *n*. It starts at the middle line and travels down. Then it curves back up the middle and comes straight down.

u

us

but

run

must

out

under

you

four

full

blue

round

would

Lowercase u

Look for the words with lowercase *u* in the word search below. Use the words in the Word Bank.

Word Bank

around	about	could	must
but	you	would	our
your	hurt	under	us
found	four	up	pull
run	full	blue	cut

a	p	a	m	u	s	t	b	p	c
r	v	c	u	t	o	d	m	u	o
o	w	x	q	e	n	p	q	l	u
u	d	y	o	u	h	t	u	l	l
n	d	a	o	f	o	u	r	d	d
d	c	f	a	y	o	u	r	p	b
e	b	u	b	a	b	o	u	t	l
b	a	l	c	o	u	r	n	t	u
u	u	l	u	n	d	e	r	p	e
t	p	w	o	u	l	d	a	u	s

Lowercase p

Lowercase *p* starts at the middle line and goes straight down. Then it comes back up and curves around to join the line at the bottom.

p

play   pretty

help   sleep

stop   keep

pick   put

Lowercase p

Read the sentences below. Complete the puzzle using the words in the Word Bank.

Down

1. A red traffic light means ____ .

2. This word means the same as beautiful.

3. This word can also mean choose.

Across

3. This word rhymes with day.

4. To make easier or assist.

5. Another word for rest.

6. A four-letter word that rhymes with sleep.

Word Bank

pretty   play

stop   keep

pick   help

sleep

Lowercase b

The lowercase *b* starts like an *l* but then goes back up to the middle line to form a circle in front.

Hint: To help tell the difference between the *b* and the *d*, try to make a capital *B* out of the lowercase *b*. If you can, then you have the *b* and not the *d*.

b

bring

big

black

better

both

before

brown

buy

be

by

Name_____ Date _____

Lowercase b

Read the words with *b* in the box below. Decide which sentence each word fits best in. Write the words on the line.

```
┌─────────────────────────────────────────────┐
│                 Word Bank                     │
│   bring     before     big      brown         │
│   black     buy        by       both          │
└─────────────────────────────────────────────┘
```

1. Don't forget to _____ your towel for the pool.

2. The store has many things to _____.

3. The coat hanger is _____ the door.

4. We are _____ going to the party.

5. The opposite of _____ is small.

6. The bear was _____ and _____.

7. Sam brushes his teeth _____ he goes to bed.

0-7682-3442-5 *Handwriting With Sight Words*

Lowercase j

Let's make a lowercase *j*.
The lowercase *j* is like the *i*, but it hangs down
like a cat's tail and is topped with a dot like
the *i*.

j

jump

just

jelly

jet

job

just

Lowercase j

Pick five words from page 50. Write a sentence for each word.

1. _____

2. _____

3. _____

4. _____

5. _____

Draw a picture to go with one of your sentences.

```



```

Lowercase q

We are going to work on our last lowercase letter, the letter *q*. Did you know that almost every word that starts with a *q* is almost always followed by a *u*? A *q* starts like a *c*, but it goes all the way back up to close the *c* and curves back down to add a tail.

q

quiz

quiet

queen

quick

quit

Name_____ Date_____

Lowercase q

Read the letter below. Practice writing it on the lines.

Dear Mom and Dad,

We just finished learning about

---

lowercase letters. We are going to have a

---

quiz on writing them all. Our teacher will

---

give us the sound each letter makes and ask

---

us to write the letter. Wish me luck!

Love,

Juan

Review of Lowercase p, r, n, m, h, b

Practice writing the letters below.

p

r

n

m

h

b

Review of Lowercase c, a, d, g, o

Practice writing the letters below.

c _____

a _____

d _____

g _____

o _____

Review of Lowercase u, i, e, l, k, y, x

Practice writing the letters below.

u

i

e

l

k

y

x

Review of Lowercase f, j, q, s, t, v, w, z

Practice writing the letters below.

f

j

q

s

t

v

w

z

Name _____   Date _____

Spacing

Look at the sentences below. What is wrong with them? Write each sentence
the way it should be written.

Thesewordsdonothaveanyspaces.

_____
- -
_____

These   words   have   too   many   spaces .

_____
- -
_____

A   pinky finger   spaceis perfect   between   words.

_____
- -
_____

When   youtype you   putonespace   between   words.

_____
- -
_____

Published by Frank Schaffer Publications. Copyright protected.   0-7682-3442-5 *Handwriting With Sight Words*

Spacing

What is wrong with letters in the sentences below? Rewrite the words the correct way on the lines below.

These lettersneedtob

eclor   t o g e t her.

This is the way the letters should be written.

Don't use spaces between letters when they

are in a word, just a space between words.

Capitalization

This is a capital *B*. This is a lowercase *b*. Most of the time we use lowercase letters when we write, but sometimes we use capital letters.

1. We always start a sentence with a capital letter.

Example: The dog went for a walk.

2. We always begin names with a capital letter.

Example: Sara went to the store.

3. We also use capital letters when writing days of the week, months of the year, and names of places.

Examples:

Today is **T**uesday.

My birthday is in **A**pril.

I live in the state of **M**ichigan.

Capitalization

Use capital letters as you complete the sentences below.

My name is

My favorite day of the week is

My friend's name is

I live in the state of

My birthday is on

Write your own sentence on the lines below. Make sure to use capital letters.

Punctuation

Let's review three important punctuation marks that we use often in writing.

This is a period: **.** It is used to end a sentence.

Example: I can read and write**.**

This is a question mark: **?** It is used to ask a question.

Example: Do you like ice cream**?**

This is an exclamation point: **!** This mark tells the reader to read with excitement in his or her voice.

Example: I love to eat pizza**!**

Punctuation

Write a sentence for each punctuation mark below.

.

?

!

Rewrite the following sentences with the correct punctuation marks and capitalization.

a period lets the reader know to pause

look, there is a fire

what is your favorite snack

where do you live

my dog's name is muffin

Answer Key

Page 17—1. two, 2. to, 3. too, 4. it, 5. cost

Page 19—

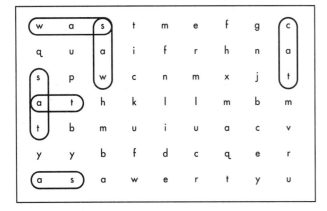

Page 21—dog, dogs, give, big, dogs, wagging, dogs, dogs, dogs, great

Page 23—1. said, 2. six, 3. sit, 4. did, 5. is, 6. It

Page 25—1. ate, 2. does, 3. eat, 4. gave, 5. get, 6. give, 7. goes, 8. see, 9. we

Page 27—Answers will vary.

Page 29—**Down:** 1. little, 2. old, 3. all, 4. will; **Across:** 1. let, 4. well, 5. tell, 6. call

Page 33—1. Look, 2. kick, 3. walk, 4. like, 5. ask, 6. skate

Page 39—1. always, 2. carry, 3. every, 4. funny, 5. say, 6. today, 7. try, 8. very, 9. why, 10. yes

Page 41—a: ran, want, and, nap; e: seven, never, went, ten; i: in, think, into, spin; o: not, long, down, on; u: under, fun, ugly, run

Page 43—**short vowels:** small, come, him, am, them; **long vowels**: make, made, my, may, me

Page 45—

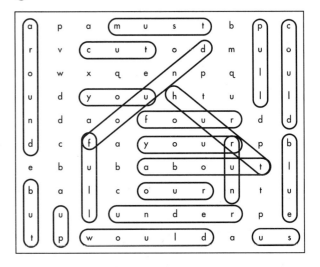

Page 47—**Down:** 1. stop, 2. pretty, 3. pick; **Across:** 3. play, 4. help, 5. sleep, 6. keep

Page 49—1. bring; 2. buy; 3. by; 4. both; 5. big; 6. brown, black; 7. before

Published by Frank Schaffer Publications. Copyright protected.   0-7682-3442-5 *Handwriting With Sight Words*